How to Be a HERO

BULLY

We hope that you find this book from _The ORP Library_ valuable.

If this book touched you in a way that you would be willing to share, we encourage you to visit www.Amazon.com or www.BN.com and write a short review.

www.ORPLibrary.com

Writers of the Round Table Press
PO Box 511
Highland Park, IL 60035

Illustration SHANE CLESTER
Publisher COREY MICHAEL BLAKE
Post Production SUNNY DIMARTINO
Director of Operations KRISTIN WESTBERG
Facts Keeper MIKE WINICOUR
Front Cover Design SHANE CLESTER, SUNNY DIMARTINO
Interior Design and Layout SUNNY DIMARTINO
Proofreading RITA HESS
Last Looks SUNNY DIMARTINO
Digital Publishing SUNNY DIMARTINO

Printed in the United States of America

First Edition: September 2014
10 9 8 7 6 5 4 3 2 1

Library of Congress Cataloging-in-Publication Data
Clester, Shane
How to be a hero: a comic book about bullying /
Shane Clester and Kristin Westberg
with Jeff Krukar, Pamela DeLoatch, and James G. Balestrieri.—1st ed. p. cm.
Print ISBN: 978-1-939418-61-6   Digital ISBN: 978-1-939418-62-3
Library of Congress Control Number: 2014945719
Number 11 in the series: The ORP Library
The ORP Library: How to Be a Hero

RTC Publishing is an imprint of Writers of the Round Table, Inc.
Writers of the Round Table Press and the RTC Publishing logo
are trademarks of Writers of the Round Table, Inc.

How to Be a Hero

A COMIC BOOK ABOUT BULLYING

THE ORP LIBRARY

WRITTEN BY
SHANE CLESTER
KRISTIN WESTBERG

ILLUSTRATED BY
SHANE CLESTER

WITH
JEFF KRUKAR, PH.D.
PAMELA DeLOATCH
JAMES G. BALESTRIERI

INTRODUCTION

I have led Oconomowoc Residential Programs (ORP) for almost thirty years. We're a family of companies offering specialized services and care for children, adolescents, and adults with disabilities. Too often, when parents of children with disabilities try to find funding for programs like ours, they are bombarded by red tape, conflicting information, or no information at all, so they struggle blindly for years to secure an appropriate education. Meanwhile, home life, and the child's wellbeing, suffers. In cases when parents and caretakers have exhausted their options—and their hope—ORP is here to help. We felt it was time to offer parents a new, unexpected tool to fight back: stories that educate, empower, and inspire.

The original idea was to create a library of comic books that could empower families with information to reclaim their rights. We wanted to give parents and caretakers the information they need to advocate for themselves, as well as provide educators and therapists with a therapeutic tool. And, of course, we wanted to reach the children—to offer them a visual representation of their journey that would show that they aren't alone, nor are they wrong or "bad" for their differences.

What we found in the process of writing original stories for the comics is that these journeys are too long, too complex, to be contained within a standard comic. So what we are now creating is an ORP library of disabilities books—traditional books geared toward parents, care-takers, educators, and therapists, *and* comic books like this one that portray the world through the eyes of chil-dren with disabilities. Both styles of books share what we have learned while advocating for families over the years while also honestly highlighting their emotional journeys.

In an ideal situation, this companion children's book will be used therapeutically, to communicate directly with these amazing children, and to help support the work ORP and companies like ours are doing. These books are the best I have to offer and if they even help a handful of people the effort will have been worth it.

Sincerely,

Jim Balestrieri
CEO, *Oconomowoc Residential Programs*

A NOTE ABOUT THIS BOOK

What exactly is bullying? Its scope is broad, and it is sometimes difficult to recognize. Bullying can range from obvious physical threats, intimidation, or abuse to more subtle emotional and psychological bullying, such as derisive notes or texts sent in class; embarrassing photos, videos, or comments posted online; or intentional shunning or exclusion. Even more important, who is a bully? Is it just the person with the aggressive behavior, or could it also include the bystanders who do nothing while the bullying continues? Understanding what bullying is, why bullying happens, and what to do, whether you are the one bullying, the one being bullied, or the observer, is key to effectively ending the behavior and addressing the pain felt by all involved. We hope that this book will raise awareness of the complexity of the issue, as well as—most importantly—offer actionable strategies for parents, educators, and children to help put an end to *all* forms of bullying.

ACCORDING TO STOPBULLYING.GOV, NEARLY ONE IN THREE AMERICAN SCHOOL CHILDREN IN GRADES SIX THOUGH TEN REPORT EXPERIENCING HARASSMENT FROM OTHER CHILDREN.

WHAT IS BULLYING?

GETTING PICKED LAST FOR TEAMS?

AW, MAN. **NO.**

GETTING PUMMELED BY EVERYONE ON BOTH TEAMS?

POP POP POP **YES!**

NOT BEING INVITED TO A PARTY OR BEING LEFT OUT OF A GAME OCCASIONALLY IS NOT CONSIDERED BULLYING. (THAT DOESN'T MEAN YOUR FEELINGS AREN'T HURT, THOUGH.)

BEING CALLED A NAME?

DORK. ?

NO.

BEING CALLED A NAME CONSTANTLY AND REPEATEDLY?

DORK. DORK. DOOOORK. DORK. DORK DORK. DORK. COME ON!

YES!

RUDE THINGS ARE SAID, AND SOMETIMES PEOPLE CAN BE MEAN, BUT BULLYING IS SOMETHING THAT IS REPEATED AND HAPPENS NUMEROUS TIMES OR CONTINUES TO HAPPEN.

THAT'S WHY IT IS IMPORTANT TO COMMUNICATE IF AND WHEN YOU ARE FEELING BULLIED OR HARASSED, SO THE BEHAVIOR CAN BE STOPPED.

BULLYING IS UNWANTED AND AGGRESSIVE BEHAVIOR
THAT INVOLVES A REAL OR PERCEIVED POWER IMBALANCE.

EVERYONE PLAYS A ROLE IN BULLYING

PERSON DOING THE BULLYING

BULLIER

PERSON WHO IS BEING BULLIED

BULLIED

PEOPLE WHO WITNESS AND OBSERVE BULLYING

BYSTANDERS

WHO ARE PEOPLE WHO BULLY?

PEOPLE WHO BULLY COME IN ALL SHAPES AND SIZES

THE KID THAT'S BULLIED TODAY...

WHAT DO YOU THINK YOU ARE DOING?

THIS IS MY COURT, SISSY.

...COULD BULLY SOMEONE TOMORROW.

HA HA! THAT'S NOT HOW YOU SPELL THAT WORD, YOU IDIOT!

MOST PEOPLE WHO BULLY ARE INSECURE AND ARE LOOKING FOR SOME TYPE OF VALIDATION THEY DON'T FEEL THEY HAVE. THEY TRY TO GET THAT FEELING BY MAKING SOMEONE ELSE FEEL BAD.

ONE THING THAT ALL PEOPLE WHO BULLY HAVE IN COMMON IS THEIR DESIRE FOR POWER AND CONTROL WITH LITTLE CONCERN FOR THE FEELINGS OF OTHERS.

THEY STRUGGLE WITH EMPATHY, THE ABILITY TO UNDERSTAND AND RELATE TO HOW ANOTHER PERSON IS FEELING.

BULLIES OFTEN THRIVE ON CONTROL—THEY WANT TO DOMINATE OTHERS AND USE THEIR POWER TO OBTAIN WHAT THEY WANT.

HAVE YOU BULLIED?

Have you often laughed when someone gets hurt or embarrassed?

Have you sent rude, embarrassing, or threatening texts or emails?

Do you enjoy making jokes about people based on their race, culture, or preferences?

Have you forced someone to do something he did not want to do?

Do you stand by and watch as someone else is bullied?

IF YOU ANSWERED "YES" TO ANY OF THESE...

YOU MIGHT BE SOMEONE WHO BULLIES.

MANY PEOPLE ARE EMBARRASSED, ASHAMED, OR EVEN SCARED TO ADMIT THEY WERE BULLIED.

BUT **ANYONE** CAN BE BULLIED.

LOSER!

NERD!

SNOB!

TRAILER TRASH!

THERE ARE 4 TYPES OF BYSTANDERS:

THE OUTSIDERS

THESE BYSTANDERS REMAIN SEPARATE FROM THE SITUATION. THEY SUPPORT THE BULLYING BEHAVIOR BY NOT INTERVENING OR DEFENDING THE PERSON BEING BULLIED.

HEROES

THESE BYSTANDERS ACTIVELY SUPPORT THE PERSON BEING BULLIED AND MAY EVEN COME TO THEIR DEFENSE.

THEY ARE THE ONES WHO DARE TO SPEAK UP, DO THE RIGHT THING, AND HELP OTHERS WHEN THEY NEED IT.

OH, NO. I'M NOT SITTING NEXT TO THE DORK!

RUDE! COME ON, YOU CAN SIT BY US.

WHY IS BULLYING A BIG DEAL?

BECAUSE BULLYING AFFECTS EVERYONE! IT AFFECTS THOSE WHO ARE BEING BULLIED, THOSE WHO ARE DOING THE BULLYING, AND THOSE WHO WITNESS THE BULLYING HAPPENING AROUND THEM. IT AFFECTS EVERYONE IN DIFFERENT WAYS.

PEOPLE WHO ARE BULLIED OFTEN FEEL:

AFRAID · UNSAFE · HOPELESS · ALONE · STRESSED

ASHAMED · CONFUSED · DEPRESSED · REJECTED · GUILTY

You may be surprised to find out that people who bully often have the same feelings as people who are bullied.

PEOPLE WHO BULLY CAN OFTEN FEEL:

AFRAID	UNSAFE	HOPELESS	ALONE	STRESSED

ASHAMED	CONFUSED	DEPRESSED	REJECTED	GUILTY

INDIRECT EFFECTS OF BULLYING

(EVEN IF YOU ARE NOT THE ONE BEING BULLIED, WITNESSING OTHERS BEING HURT CAN CAUSE YOU TO EXPERIENCE MANY OF THESE EFFECTS.)

WHAT CAN YOU DO IF YOU ARE BEING BULLIED?

DON'T BELIEVE WHAT THE BULLY SAYS ABOUT YOU.

DON'T CALL ME STUPID. I JUST GOT AN A+!

BE PROUD OF YOURSELF.

HEY KID, WHAT ARE YOU DOING? BOYS DON'T PLAY WITH UNICORNS!

I DO!

STAY CALM.

PEOPLE WHO ARE BULLYING OFTEN PICK ON PEOPLE THEY KNOW THEY CAN GET A REACTION OUT OF. WHEN YOU OVERREACT OR CAUSE A SCENE, THEY FEEL POWERFUL BECAUSE THEY CAUSED THAT REACTION.

FAKE IT.

EVEN IF YOU AREN'T FEELING BRAVE AND STRONG, FAKE IT. IT IS CRITICAL THAT THE PERSON BULLYING YOU THINKS THAT YOU ARE. YOU CAN LET OUT YOUR FEELINGS AND DISCUSS YOUR EMOTION WITH AN ADULT OR TRUSTED SUPPORT PERSON AT A LATER TIME.

AVOID PUTTING YOURSELF IN A SITUATION WHERE YOU ARE ALONE WITH SOMEONE WHO BULLIES.

SURROUND YOURSELF WITH FRIENDS AND PEOPLE WHO CARE ABOUT YOU.

WHAT CAN YOU DO IF YOU SEE OTHERS BEING BULLIED?

SPEAK UP FOR THEM.

HEY!

LEAVE THAT KID ALONE!

IF YOU BULLIED OR WERE BULLIED BY ANOTHER, WILL YOU LOOK BACK ON YOUR LIFE AND WISH YOU HAD ACTED DIFFERENTLY?

WILL YOU WISH YOU HAD TOLD SOMEONE?

WILL YOU REALIZE WHAT HAPPENED TO BULLIED KIDS WASN'T FUNNY?

WILL YOU FEEL GUILTY FOR TORMENTING OTHERS?

NOW IS THE TIME TO THINK ABOUT THESE QUESTIONS—TO STOP AND THINK ABOUT HOW YOU HAVE BEEN ACTING TOWARDS OTHERS AND TOWARD YOURSELF.

YOU **CAN** MAKE A DIFFERENCE AND CHANGE THE BULLYING CULTURE IN YOUR COMMUNITY.

EACH DAY, SOMEONE IS BULLIED IN THE PRESENCE OF BYSTANDERS, IN FRONT OF PEOPLE WHO CAN POTENTIALLY MAKE A DIFFERENCE IF THEY CHOOSE NOT TO BE SILENT AND JUST OBSERVE THE BULLYING.

ANYONE CAN BE A HERO.

CLASSMATE.

BROTHER OR SISTER.

TEACHER.

FRIEND.

COACH.

PARENT.

STEP UP. BE A HERO.

BULLY

Hero

he·ro
ˈhi(ə)rō/
noun
plural: heroes
1. a person who is admired or idealized for courage, outstanding achievements, or noble qualities.

HOW THESE BOOKS WERE CREATED

The ORP Library of disabilities books is the result of heartfelt collaboration between numerous people: the staff of ORP, including the CEO, executive director, psychologists, clinical coordinators, teachers, and more; the families of children with disabilities served by ORP, including some of the children themselves; and the Round Table Companies (RTC) storytelling team. To create these books, RTC conducted dozens of intensive, intimate interviews over a period of months and performed independent research in order to truthfully and accurately depict the lives of these families. We are grateful to all those who donated their time in support of this message, generously sharing their experience, wisdom, and—most importantly—their stories so that the books will ring true. While each story is fictional and not based on any one family or child, we could not have envisioned the world through their eyes without the access we were so lovingly given. It is our hope that in reading this uniquely personal book, you felt the spirit of everyone who contributed to its creation.

ACKNOWLEDGMENTS

The authors would like to thank Jen and Rod Anderson, Joan Baguhn, Dr. John Dominguez, Cindy Fleiss, Julie Hohenwald, Jackie Paullin, and Julie Yeager-Preilwitz for their insights and contributions. Thank you for both helping to illuminate the scope of the bullying problem and for being part of the solution.

RESOURCES

Anderson, Connie, Ph.D. "IAN Research Report: Bullying and Children with ASD." Interactive Autism Network. *http://www .iancommunity.org/cs/ian_research_reports/ian_research_report _bullying.*

Anthes, Emily. "Inside the Bullied Brain." *The Boston Globe*, November 28, 2010, *http://www.boston.com/bostonglobe/ideas /articles/2010/11/28/inside_the_bullied_brain.*

Dominguez, John. "Tackling Peer Harassment." *Quintessential Barrington*, Sept–Oct. 2012, 48.

Fields, R. Douglas. "The New Brain." *Psychology Today*, October 30, 2010, *http://www.psychologytoday.com/blog/the-new-brain /201010/sticks-and-stones-hurtful-words-damage-the-brain.*

Massachusetts Advocates for Children. "Targeted, Taunted, Tormented: The Bullying of Children with Autism Spectrum Disorder." *http://www.massadvocates.org/documents/Bullying-Report _000.pdf.*

Melloy, Kilian. "Your Brain on Bullying." *Edge Boston*, March 21, 2011, *http://www.edgeboston.com/columnists/kilian_melloy/// 117045/your_brain_on_bullying.*

PACER's National Bullying Prevention Center. "Peer Advocacy." *http://www.pacer.org/bullying/resources/students-with-disabilities /peer-advocacy.asp.*

StopBullying.gov. "Bullying Statistics in America." *http://www .nobullying.com/bullying-statistics.*

StopBullying.gov. "What is Bullying." *http://www.stopbullying.gov /what-is-bullying/definition/index.html.*

University of Rochester Medical Center. "Children With Both Autism And ADHD Often Bully, Parents Say: Researchers Caution Against Labeling." *ScienceDaily*, May 18, 2007, *http:// www.sciencedaily.com/releases/2007/05/070517100417.htm.*

Walsh, David. "The Bullied Brain." *Huffington Post*, August 1, 2011, *http://www.huffingtonpost.com/david-walsh/the-bullied-brain_b _914709.html*, 8/1/11.

"About the Bully Project," The Bully Project, accessed July 29, 2013, *http://www.thebullyproject.com/about_the_bully_project.*

BIOGRAPHIES

As a child, Shane Clester loved drawing. Robots, ninjas, He-Man figures, lyrics from Lionel Richie songs; Shane drew everything. He was either going to be an astronaut or an artist when he grew up, or a ninja robot fighting astronaut. Finding out later that he didn't have the eyesight to be an astronaut, and that a ninja robot fighting astronaut wasn't a real thing, he pursued his art. He worked a virtual cornucopia of odd jobs before becoming a professional doodle monkey. Shane has had a varied and fulfilling career so far and looks forward to the day when, as an old man, he looks out the window of his moon base reflecting back on his life. But for now, Shane lives in sunny southern Florida with his cutie pie wife, hilarious baby girl, snuggly pets, and reasonably sized action figure collection; hoping each time that his next leap will be his leap home.

With nine years of middle school teaching experience as well as an M.S. in Youth Development Leadership and a M.Ed. in Higher Ed Administration, Kristin Westberg thoroughly understands the practice and theory of creating an environment that is intolerant of bullying. As part of her role as RTC's director of operations, Kristin designs curriculum and creates workbooks and other teaching tools. Her work with this comic book is a culmination of her varied expertise. As her own children progress through school, Kristin tries to instill the lessons in this comic book in them, in hopes that they will be "upstanders"—unwilling to ignore, encourage, or tolerate bullying.

Jeffrey D. Krukar, Ph.D. is a licensed psychologist and certified school psychologist with more than 20 years of experience working with children and families in a variety of settings. As the psychologist at Genesee Lake School in Oconomowoc, WI, Dr. Krukar hopes the ORP Library of disabilities books will bring stories of children and families to a world that is generally not aware of their challenges and successes, as well as offer a sense of hope to those currently on this journey.

Pamela DeLoatch is a writer, editor, and storyteller. Drawing on her journalism and business degrees, she crafts writing that educates, entertains, and engages. For eight months, Pamela immersed herself in the story of a boy named Jason, creating the first book about bullying in the ORP Library, *Classroom Heroes*, exploring how those around him challenged the pervasiveness of bullying by changing their concept of individual accountability. She hopes her work makes a difference.

James G. Balestrieri is currently the CEO of Oconomowoc Residential Programs, Inc. (ORP). He has worked in the human services field for 40 years, gaining experience in nearly every area. With a passion for creatively addressing the needs of those with impairments by managing the inherent stress among funding, programming, and profitability, Jim believes that people with disabilities have a right to find their place in the world and to achieve their maximum potential as individuals. For more information, see *www.orp.com*.

ABOUT ORP

Oconomowoc Residential Programs, Inc. is an employee-owned family of companies whose mission is to make a difference in the lives of people with disabilities. Our dedicated staff of 2,000 employee owners provides quality services and professional care to more than 1,700 children, adolescents, and adults with special needs. ORP provides a continuum of care, including residential therapeutic education, community-based residential services, support services, respite care, treatment programs, and day services. The individuals in our care include people with developmental disabilities, physical disabilities, and intellectual disabilities. **Our guiding principle is passion:** a passion for the people we serve and for the work we do. For a comprehensive look at our programs and people, please visit *www.orp.com.*

ORP offers residential therapeutic education programs and alternative day schools among its array of services. These programs offer developmentally appropriate education and treatment for children, adolescents, and young adults in settings specially attuned to their needs. We provide special programs for students with specific academic and social issues relative to a wide range of disabilities, including autistic disorder, Asperger's disorder, mental retardation, anxiety disorders, depression, bipolar disorder, reactive attachment disorder, attention deficit disorder, Prader-Willi Syndrome, and other disabilities.

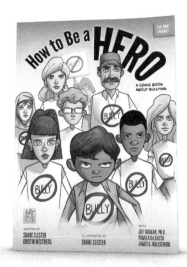

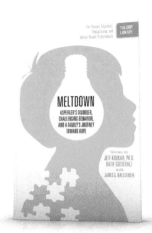

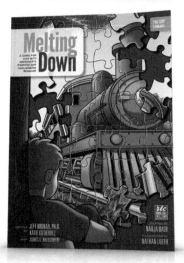

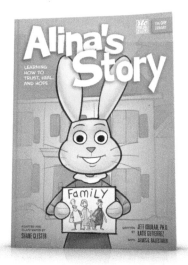

AN UNLIKELY TRUST
ALINA'S STORY OF ADOPTION, COMPLEX TRAUMA, HEALING, AND HOPE

JEFF KRUKAR, PH.D.
KATIE GUTIERREZ
with
JAMES G. BALESTRIERI

Alina's Story
LEARNING HOW TO TRUST, HEAL, AND HOPE

ADAPTED AND ILLUSTRATED BY
SHANE CLESTER

WRITTEN BY JEFF KRUKAR, PH.D.
KATIE GUTIERREZ
with JAMES G. BALESTRIERI

INSATIABLE
A PRADER-WILLI STORY

Written by
DEBBIE FRISK
CHELSEA McCUTCHIN
with
JAMES G. BALESTRIERI
KATIE GUTIERREZ

Ultra-Violet
ONE GIRL'S PRADER-WILLI STORY

ILLUSTRATED BY
NATHAN LUETH
WRITTEN BY
CHELSEA McCUTCHIN
DEBBIE FRISK
with
JAMES G. BALESTRIERI

CHASING HOPE
YOUR COMPASS FOR A NEW NORMAL

NAVIGATING THE WORLD OF THE SPECIAL NEEDS CHILD

Written by
CHRISTINE WALKER

Also look for books on children and psychotropic medications coming soon!

CPSIA information can be obtained at www.ICGtesting.com
Printed in the USA
LVOW02s1038050914

402583LV00001B/1/P

9 781939 418616